The
Amazing
Golden
Years

THE AMAZING GOLDEN YEARS

CALVIN L. EMERSON

REMEMBER:
WHAT GOD HAS DONE IN YOUR PAST
AND
YOU WILL TRUST HIM MORE IN YOUR FUTURE

XULON PRESS

Xulon Press
2301 Lucien Way #415
Maitland, FL 32751
407.339.4217
www.xulonpress.com

© 2019 by Calvin L. Emerson

All rights reserved solely by the author. The author guarantees all contents are original and do not infringe upon the legal rights of any other person or work. No part of this book may be reproduced in any form without the permission of the author. The views expressed in this book are not necessarily those of the publisher.

Unless otherwise indicated, Scripture quotations taken from the Holy Bible, New International Version (NIV). Copyright © 1973, 1978, 1984, 2011 by Biblica, Inc.™. Used by permission. All rights reserved.

Printed in the United States of America.

ISBN-13: 978-154566-996-9

I WOULD LIKE TO THANK MY WIFE, **Beverly**. I do not type, so she spent hours typing for me, questioning my thought progressions, and the whole time going half-blind reading between the lines, up the left and right indents, and wondering what my misspelled words meant. She has been very patient and encouraging when I was ready to give up. I could not have done this without her. She is a blessing from God.

I am also thankful for **Pam Coffey**. Pam did the initial editing for me and made some very embarrassing corrections. I have used Pam for three of my past books and am so thankful that she is using her God-given ability to work behind the scenes. She is a dear friend and a sister in Christ.

I am so proud that my grandson, **Jake White**, did a read-through and made some suggestions that helped the stories flow more smoothly. Jake recently graduated with a degree in English Literature from the University of Colorado. He is my oldest grandson, and I'm sure he is on the way to a very successful career. Thank you, Jake.

TABLE OF CONTENTS

Introduction: The Amazing Golden Years ix

Chapter 1: The Most Embarrassing
Moment of My Life. 1

Chapter 2: Embarrassment Becomes Positive 9

Chapter 3: Then My Life Became Even Richer . . 19

Chapter 4: Change Brought Difficulties 26

Chapter 5: The Difficulties Got Worse 33

Chapter 6: The Trials Keep Coming 42

Chapter 7: The Failed Cottage Plan 51

Chapter 8: The Blessings My Family Gave Me . . 60

Chapter 9: A More Recent Lesson 70

Chapter 10: House Fire 80

Chapter 11: Why I Was Never Pastor
of a Big Church 89

Chapter 12: God's Sense of Humor 98

Chapter 13: Remember 106

Introduction

The Amazing Golden Years

I'm not here to try to convince you that the golden years are without pain, sorrow, and some disappointments. If that is the message you are looking for, then I suggest you go back to the bookstore and purchase another book. This is not a book about the wonders of retirement or traveling around the world or spending your winters in Florida. The golden years are the years when my body and I are not in agreement with each other. They are the years when a big part of my social life is simply striking up conversations with strangers in the waiting rooms of doctors' offices. In my golden years, I seem to have more social life than ever before.

I have cancer, macular degeneration, arthritis, peripheral neuropathy, and two prosthetic hips. My body has been falling apart for twenty some years now.

I struggle to remember words while conversing with others. When writing, I sometimes leave a space blank for the perfect word that is out there somewhere. I thank God that I can usually fill in that blank sometime during my first, second, or even third time through the editing process. My mind is not as quick as it used to be. I can come up with some answers to the questions on *Jeopardy!* but am usually late on the buzzer because the answers come two to three days later.

This is not a book from Norman Vincent Peale suggesting that the golden years can be perfect if we just think more positively. Rather, it is a book that defines the joy of aging and the beauty of the aging process. It is a book looking back at the wonders of life and the fulfilling lessons we have learned along the way. If we can do that, we can then see God's hand on our lives through every crisis, every trouble, every disappointment, and every trial. These lessons are not detectable when we are experiencing troubles and difficult times. It is hard to see the positive outcome of a difficult situation while we are suffocating in the middle of it. They are things we can only see as we look back and realize we have successfully navigated every tragedy that seemed to be insurmountable at the time.

The Amazing Golden Years

This is a book about the wonderful lessons I have learned as I endured trials and difficulties. The only way I can write this book is to use my personal experiences and share the lessons I have learned. You have not experienced the same trials, but hopefully mine will stimulate your mind and help you evaluate the ups and downs in your life. Then, with the help of scriptures used and study questions at the end of each chapter, I pray that God may open your mind and reveal the way He has worked in your life when you thought He was ignoring you. Once you do that, the golden years become a whole lot more golden.

The next three chapters will explain the most exciting part of my life. Even though the first one will reveal my most embarrassing moment, you will see that chapter two defines that moment, and I hope it will put the remaining chapters into perspective.

The Bible verse that best defines the purpose of this book is a conversation between Moses and his father-in-law, Jethro. Moses shares all the difficulties he experienced while trying to free the Israelites from Egypt.

> "He [Moses] also told [Jethro, his father-in-law] about all the hardships they had experienced along the way and how the

Lord had rescued His people from all their troubles." Exodus 18:8b NLT

As Moses shares all the wonders God performed to deliver the Israelites, Jethro viewed God on a much grander scale. The next verse states that Jethro was delighted to hear all the good things the Lord had done for Moses and the Israelites. It also states that Jethro was encouraged to serve the great God who had delivered Moses. As I share what God has done in my life and the lessons I have learned, I hope you will respond in a similar manner. If you can do so, then you will also begin to call your retirement years the amazing golden years.

Study Questions:

1. Name a time in your life when you made it through a difficult situation.
2. As you look back, how do you see God working in that trial?
3. What were your emotions as you traversed this trial? Defeat, anger, hopelessness, depression?
4. What could the outcome have been had the Lord not been involved?

Chapter 1

The Most Embarrassing Moment of My Life

This chapter and the next will begin to define why I am writing this book. In them I will talk about my spiritual journey and the events that took place to eventually lead me into the ministry.

I was a junior in high school, and it was a week before homecoming. As I ran out of the locker room, excited to play the second half of the football game, the varsity club was doing a skit to promote homecoming. I knew what the promotion was about but had no idea how much it would overwhelm me emotionally.

There, driving around the track in front of the guest bleachers and then the home bleachers, was a rusty old limousine. It stopped in front of the home stands and the shortest guy in the senior class got out dressed up in a tuxedo. He opened the back door of the limo and helped Ralph, the tallest guy in the senior class, get out of the car. Ralph was dressed in a strapless evening gown with hairy legs showing.

The audience could not hold back the laughter, as it was a sight to behold. The emcee interviewed the couple, and the tall guy/girl spoke with a farm drawl indicating he was just grateful that he got the cows milked in time to get there. The short guy commented that he should not have worn the evening gown into the barn to do the milking, as it smelled like cow. The tall guy even said he had been practicing for years to become the queen. When asked how, he said he only milked every other cow so he could get done on time.

The five-minute discourse was hilarious, and the crowd roared. Yet it was the most embarrassing time in my life because that rusty old limo was our family car. We were a family of eight, and my dad had a two-year college degree and an amazing work ethic. He just never earned a lot of money. Dad was able to buy that large family car very cheap because no one else would be caught dead in it. At least that is how I felt.

As I watched the halftime scenario unfold, I felt the whole town was laughing at my family and how poor we were. How embarrassing. It was okay to drive the car to church or even town, because then only a few people would see us at one time. But that evening the whole town was there, and every one of them was laughing. After that evening I made a vow never to embarrass my future family as my family had embarrassed me. I would do whatever it took to earn a decent living and purchase acceptable cars.

To overcome the immediate embarrassment, however, my brother and I did something I don't think our mother ever forgave us for. It was an era when teenage guys with hot cars named their cars. They would paint names like "Temptation" or "Lightning" on the back fenders just to express their power and beauty. Those were the cars of the sixties that were so powerful they would vibrate when they idled at a red light. When they were revved up, store windows would break from the vibration (or at least that's how it seemed).

We obviously didn't have a hot car, but we named the ugly limo anyway. Since the funeral homes were the only ones in our small town that owned a limo, we agreed on the name "The Last Ride," and yes, we painted it on both back fenders. It was our way of laughing at ourselves so that the community laughter wouldn't hurt so much. Oh, was Mom upset. I'm not sure she ever drove that car to town again.

1950 DeSoto limousine

There are two lessons I learned here, but I didn't realize each one until many years later as a result of that rusty old limo. The first was to work hard so I could afford a nice car. I was able to secure an unbelievable job after college and was able to purchase a brand-new 1974 Oldsmobile 98. That car was so big I would have to feed two parking meters if I parallel parked it or block one lane of traffic if I parked it on an angle. It was beautiful.

It had a 455-cubic-inch engine and wouldn't settle down and cruise until around 85 mph. I had to keep telling my wife to slow down. I had a lot of trouble holding it back on those two-lane country roads and, consequently, was pulled over by police a few times. The gas mileage was terrible but would probably have improved were I able to keep my right foot out of the carburetor. It was a beautiful car. I was not ashamed to have anyone see me driving that car.

The next three cars I owned were the German-made Mercedes-Benz. They were prestigious cars. There was never an embarrassing moment driving those three vehicles. In fact, I could just imagine people were looking at me in envy as I passed them by. I always tried to be cool about it and not look to see if that was happening, even though I really wanted to. The parts to the Mercedes were so well engineered that it gave me great pleasure to tell first-time passengers, "There is no need to slam the door."

My second Mercedes was orange, and it did stand out on the highway. I'm sure that made people gaze my way. That was the time before cell phones, so I had a mobile phone installed. It was very expensive, and there were very few people who could afford them. I rationalized that I could save time with the phone by using my car as a traveling office.

The phone was quite useless because there were miles and miles of highway travel where there was no reception. I had to be near a big city to use it. Then when I got to a big city, there were only one or two radio towers I could use to make a connection, and those were usually tied up by other mobile-phone users.

I did get a satisfying use out of the phone, however, by driving down the highway with the receiver up to my ear even if I was not able to talk. Now that made people look. No one was laughing at me anymore because of the car I drove. I then bought a third Mercedes and paid cash for it. My job was going well, and I could easily afford to do so. Owning that expensive car and paying cash for it was everything I had dreamed about. I had arrived.

In hindsight, what lesson did I learn from that rusty old limo? How did God use that incident and make it into a blessing fifteen years later? It was because of that great embarrassment that I worked very hard to become successful. I worked hard to earn enough money to buy very distinguished cars.

But the job I had did more than just enable me to buy expensive cars. It also gave me a prestigious lifestyle. I loved to tell my neighbors that I had to fly to New York or California the next day or even tell them that I had to fly to Europe on a business trip.

I had no idea how much that embarrassing moment would change my life. Back in high school I feared the embarrassment would never go away and that I would never be able to recover. But in the long run, it did go away, and I did recover. It has taken me years to look back and see the positive that would come out of something so negative, but something very positive did happen, and that is just one of the trials in my life that I can now thank God I had to go through. That embarrassing moment made me into a better person, as God has so beautifully promised in the following verse. Even though I wasn't walking with the Lord at the time, this verse later defined a lot of things in my life.

> Romans 8:28 states, "And we know that in all things God works for the good of those who love Him, who have been called according to His purpose."

God is saying that He can turn every trial, every tragedy, and every hardship in our lives into blessings as we walk with Him. He can turn every hardship around 180 degrees and turn it into a blessing when we trust Him. We may not see the blessing until years later, but it will be there. I find it very exciting to serve this God!

But the lessons I learned here take on an even greater worth as you will see in the next chapter.

Study Questions:

1. There is a beautiful promise in Romans 8:28, but there is also a condition we must meet to make this promise come true.
   a. What is the promise?
   b. What is the condition?
2. What does it mean "to be called according to His purpose"?
3. How could my life have turned out differently if it were not for that defining embarrassing moment?
4. What is a negative moment in your life that changed the course of your life?
5. How would your life have turned out differently without that moment?

Chapter 2

Embarrassment Becomes Positive

The most embarrassing moment in my life became a positive moment fifteen years later. I had to live through the embarrassment of the whole community laughing at my family because of the cars we drove. It wasn't just the rusty old limo that was the problem. We had cars with holes in the floor, allowing dust to infiltrate the interior on dusty roads. It was embarrassing to take my date home, get out of the car, and brush off the dust.

We had cars with heaters that didn't work. Kissing a date good night with a wet nose just isn't that romantic. We had cars with coffee cans wired around the mufflers to cover up the holes. That took away some of the noise but caused an awful vibration where the can touched the muffler. Plus, we sometimes sat on the side of the road while on vacation because the car broke down and refused to go one inch further. I can remember watching everyone drive by with cars that ran well. They weren't having trouble. I just thank God that my Dad was an airplane mechanic during World War II and knew how to repair broken-down cars sitting on the side of the road.

I even remember painting one of our cars with a paintbrush, trying to cover up some of the rust. Yes, I said a paintbrush. With all that emotional baggage, it's a wonder I can even act normal (some of the time). If your family always drove nice new cars, I know it's hard to relate to my emotional scars. But to me, they are real.

At my present age, I can look back over my life and see God developing me every step of the way. He knew where my life was headed but also knew it was going to take a lot of "life lessons" to get me there.

Continuing with the most embarrassing moment of my life, it came to a very positive end when I was thirty-one years old. I had just bought my third Mercedes, the one I paid cash for. Today, the check for that car would be for around $50,000. My life was complete. I had met my goal in life by buying a brand-new, expensive car and not having to go into debt for it.

Embarrassment Becomes Positive

MY MERCEDES 240D

The car was two days old and I was driving to Detroit to meet with some customers in that area. As I drove, the excitement of driving a brand-new, debt-free Mercedes seemed to be waning, as that was the third Mercedes I'd owned. I wanted to feel a great accomplishment, but instead I seemed to feel a little dull and a little less enthusiastic.

Then, about halfway to Detroit, it hit me. I started thinking, "Is this all there is in life? At the age of thirty-one, have I accomplished all my goals and dreams? Am I going to have to go through the rest of my life bored out of my mind because I have arrived? There surely has to be more to life than owning a beautiful car debt-free."

Then some haunting thoughts entered my mind and I started a conversation with myself. I thought:

> I have staked my life on driving this car down the highway—this beautiful, new, expensive car. What will it look like ten years from now? Well, it will probably have some scratches and dents on it and will very likely show some signs of rust. And this is what your life has been focused on?

> Your focus has been to own an expensive car like this. Let's evaluate your emotions. Does it love you the way you desire to be loved? Well, that's a ridiculous question. This car is four thousand pounds of steel, plastic, leather, and rubber. It's crazy to think it can love me. Get real. So, you have worked hard to buy an object that is not capable of loving you. What will you buy next to complete your life and make you even

happier? Well, I could buy a sailboat, as I enjoy sailing. So how long do you think that will make you happy? Perhaps a couple years. What then?

I've always felt slighted because some people own a cottage on a lake in northern Michigan. Now that would be a fun goal. For how long? I could possibly get five years of excitement out of that. But then at the end of five years, I would be right back at the same place I am right now. I will have spent five years that gave me momentary happiness only to sense a feeling of emptiness later.

And what about the money you are earning? Yes, you have a reasonable amount stashed away, but who says it will be there when you need it? How can you protect it? The stock market could crash. Don't put it there. The banks could close. Don't put it there. You could bury it in your backyard, but

> then it could be stolen or rot. Rumor has it that some of the large farmers in the area have stashed their money in the walls of their homes. But what if their home burns? That would be a fortune going up in flames.
>
> Your car is not exciting you, the sailboat will lose its excitement, and you admit that the cottage may become boring after five years, plus you are fearful of losing your money. Maybe it's time to introduce a whole new set of life goals. Goals that will never disappoint you and let you down. Goals that will bring you a great joy and, at the same time, goals that are achievable.

As I drove to Detroit that morning, going through those disappointing moments, I knew what my next step had to be. It was a step I absolutely refused to consider, but I knew I had to take it. I knew from being raised in a church that the only thing there was out there that could bring me joy was a life completely devoted to Jesus.

I had refused to make that decision for years because of all the laws and restrictions that would be heaped upon me. I knew I would no longer be able to do whatever I wanted to do. I would become a wallflower at gatherings when I loved getting together with people. I loved to earn money, lots of money, and that was something Jesus didn't seem to be in favor of. I loved not being poor and I loved being respected in a community. I knew that might come to an end.

But then the following verses came to mind. It was verses I remembered from Sunday school, and it defined everything I was doing wrong.

> Matthew 6:19-20 states, "Do not store up for yourselves treasures on earth, where moth and rust destroy, and where thieves break in and steal. But store up for yourselves treasures in heaven, where moth and rust do not destroy, and where thieves do not break in and steal."

These treasures on earth were the very things that gave me only momentary pleasure and joy.

No matter how my life might change, I had to make a spiritual decision. I didn't want to do it, but I had no choice. I realized there was nothing in the world that could give me lasting satisfaction. So, without stopping the car, I started to pray, "Lord Jesus, I desperately need You. Everything I have touched, every goal I have set before me has brought me little satisfaction. So now I give You the rest of my life. Come into my heart and be Lord over my actions, my thought life, and my relationships with other people. Please forgive me of my sins. The rest of my life is Yours because I desperately need You."

I don't know how to explain what happened next other than that brand-new Mercedes began to glow. It seemed that people were passing me and wondering what was happening in that car. I immediately experienced a peace in my life like I had never known before. I was no longer fearful about my money, my car rusting, or anything else. I was experiencing a greater joy than I ever thought possible in this life.

Everything was going to be okay. Everything was going to work out. Gradually, my wife became more beautiful to me and my daughter became more precious. I began to spend more time with my family. Even my home became less important, yet more beautiful. Explain that.

Embarrassment Becomes Positive

Most of those changes took place over time. I didn't recognize some of them right away, but they became obvious, as I have been able to look back over my life years later. Going back to chapter one in this book, it was that most embarrassing moment in my life that changed the rest of my life in such a beautiful way.

If you had said at the time of embarrassment that something wonderful would come of it, I would have said you were nuts. It took twelve years before I could afford my Oldsmobile 98. Twelve years! And then another three years before my life-changing experience. That is a total of fifteen years before my embarrassment turned into something positive. But I have to say now that it was well worth the wait.

That is the kind of event that helps me understand that the golden years are truly amazing. At my age today, I can look back over my life and measure the effects of event after painful event, and I am able to say that each one has become a blessing, even though it was painful or even devastating at the time.

Yet for me that was just the beginning of an even greater story, and one that reveals how I became even richer.

STUDY QUESTIONS:

1. What in your life seemed to be a great accomplishment at the time only to turn out a little less satisfying as time went by?
2. Looking at the fact that earthly accomplishments lose their luster in time, if you have never asked Jesus to be Lord of your life, why not?
3. As you think about one or two hard times you have experienced in your life, what lessons have you learned from them?
4. How does the previous verse, "And we know that in all things God works for the good of those who love Him, who are called according to His purpose" fit into your life as you recall the hard times you have experienced?

Chapter 3

Then My Life Became Even Richer

Because of that embarrassing moment in high school, my life began to change in a very positive direction. I didn't want to tell anyone about my love for Jesus in case the new direction turned out less than gratifying, just like my other ventures. Plus, what if I failed and had trouble living up the lifestyle, I had perceived God desired of me?

I set a condition on my commitment. I told God that I would try the new direction in my life for six months, and if it continued to be exciting after that time, I would pursue it even further. But until then I would not tell a soul, not even my wife.

To bring closure to that part of the journey, it was twelve months later that I was reminded of the condition I had set. It was like God was asking me, "Well, Cal, how has the journey been so far? Has it been a good experience or another disappointing one?" I'll have to admit that, even though I experienced great joy and peace when I made the commitment to become a Christian, I was experiencing an even greater amount now. This was too wonderful and exciting to let it slip away. I had made the decision having no idea how gratifying it would become. Now it was a no-brainer. I had to move forward.

Yet it was also a very confusing time in my life. Now I didn't know how to act around my friends. Should I still pursue their friendship, or should I consider them evil and shun them? Should I continue to listen to their crude jokes, or should I turn my nose up at them and walk away? Should I only hang out around Christians, or should I allow my old friends to see my newfound joy?

I began studying the Bible intently because it brought so much excitement into my life. I started attending a different church, one where I was taught Truth from the Bible. In fact, I have still failed to meet a more gifted Bible instructor than pastor Glen Pettigrove. Perhaps it was because I was so hungry to learn. Everything I heard was changing my life and giving me greater understanding of all the wonderful things God had in store for me.

Then my life became even richer seven years later. I started feeling a strange urge to do something that, from worldly standards, was very foolish. I began to sense a desire to go into the ministry and become a pastor. It was a foolish idea because I was making more money than I ever dreamed of making. Plus, I was beginning to climb the corporate ladder, and I thought going into the ministry would become a life of poverty. Was I willing to make that commitment?

None of that seemed important anymore. All I could focus on was the great honor of sharing God's Word and watching it change peoples' lives as it had changed mine. I began taking classes and within one year was offered a church. It was a very small church and it was really struggling, but it was a wonderful group of loving people. There were only fourteen people in the church, and our family increased it to a whopping nineteen. Now that is great church growth: it is thirty five percent in one year, if my math is correct. We stayed at that church for twenty-eight years and eventually retired there.

NORTHGATE CHURCH

The church looks huge, but only 20 percent of it was finished on the inside. Psalm 37:4 defines that part of my journey the best. The Bible says:

> "Delight yourself in the Lord and He will
> give you the desires of your heart"

As I went into the ministry, God did give me the desires of my heart. My previous two careers were exciting. But neither could give me the satisfaction of studying something so positive and then watching it change the lives of people I cared about.

I became a pastor and I loved it. I loved teaching God's Word. But it all can be traced back to the rusty old limo my junior year in high school. In my heart I never wanted to be laughed at again. As I graduated and started my first career, I started buying a series of nice cars. That seemed to be very important to me. There was never going to be any rusty old used cars sitting in my driveway. It gave me great pride to drive home to attend my fifteen-year class reunion in a very expensive Mercedes-Benz. But then, as mentioned in chapter two, that line of expensive cars left me less than satisfied.

My career was great, my income was wonderful, my family was doing well, but I knew I wanted more out of life than what I was experiencing. My focus was to impress people by driving expensive cars, but that focus left me feeling empty. At that point in my life, I became a Christ follower and later went into the ministry. But the journey into the ministry started with that rusty old limo.

I was unable to perceive, back in high school, how something so negative could turn into something so positive in my life. Back then, I remained embarrassed the next day and the next year and even through my college years. Yet fifty-seven years later it has all been put into perspective and I am now very thankful I had to go through it. That is what the golden years bring. They put into perspective why I had to tolerate some of my troubles and disappointments in life. Now I can look back and see that I was able to endure each one even if they seemed devastating. I love the golden years. My health is waning, but my joy and faith are growing.

Here is an overall view of my spiritual journey:

- I was embarrassed as the community laughed at our family car.
- Thus, I was determined to make a lot of money and buy expensive cars.
- Then I began to realize that earthly treasures would gradually lose their excitement.
- I became hungry to enjoy life on a grander scale.
- I became a Christian, as that was all that was left.
- I loved my new life and grew a deep desire to share it.
- That is why I went into the ministry at the age of thirty-nine.

As a footnote to the choice I made, had I not followed the prompting of the Holy Spirit, and had I not gone into the ministry, I would have lost my job with adidas within the next year. Adidas Germany opted to buy out all the United States importers and distributors and then set up their own sales force and distribution center. I would have been crowded out and may have ended up selling vacuum cleaners' door to door rather than selling the prestigious adidas line.

STUDY QUESTIONS:

1. Once again we see a promise made with a condition that must be met in Psalm 37:4.
   a. What is the promise?
   b. What is the condition?
   c. Explain the condition in your own words.
   e. How do you respond to that condition?
2. What may have been a time in your life when you chose "common sense" instead of obeying the prompting of the Holy Spirit?
3. Discuss the pros and cons of that choice.

Chapter 4

Change Brought Difficulties

Allow me to back up twelve months to help you see the growing pains we had to endure before going into the ministry. Beverly and I decided to spend a year in prayer before making the change. We wanted to make sure this was God's will for our lives and not just a midlife crisis I was going through. Sometimes I get excited about a plan without realizing that every plan must endure a number of hurdles.

The year of prayer started on my mother's birthday. The whole family was together to celebrate. Beverly and I decided to share our dreams with them. We told them that we were going to spend a year in prayer, and if it was God's will, we would go into the ministry on Mom's next birthday. Mom was very excited, but the rest of the family thought we had consumed too much wine, which was hard to do because there was no wine being served.

It was an exciting announcement no matter what the rest of the family thought. Yes, I had a wonderful career, and yes, I would make a lot less money, and yes, my first church would be very small because it would take me four years to become ordained and then another nine years to receive my master's degree. But it was hard to hold back our excitement and enthusiasm.

We went home that evening, however, and our enthusiasm came to a very abrupt stop. It was less than eight hours after sharing our dream when the year of troubles began. I spoke about the most embarrassing moment of my life. Well, this proved to be the most difficult year of my life.

After dinner that evening, I was wrestling with my youngest son, who was three years old. I noticed that he was a little more clumsy than usual. I wondered if I was just imagining things or if something was wrong. I held him up in front of me to look him over and realized that his right eye was turned in just a little. Was he becoming cross-eyed?

I put my hand over his right eye and he just looked at me and smiled as if we were playing a game. Then I covered up his left eye and John began to jerk his head away from my hand. He said to me as he freed himself from my hand, "Dad, don't turn out the lights."

It was on the day we announced we were going into the ministry that I realized my innocent; three-year-old son had gone blind in his right eye. Now that did not settle well with me at all. I was dedicating my life to do Kingdom work and God had allowed my youngest son to go blind. Is that the God I wanted to serve? I wasn't sure anymore. I have never had eight hours change one of my dreams so fast.

The next few weeks became almost unbearable. We took John to his pediatrician, and after a quick exam, he called a leading ophthalmologist and got him an appointment right away. That was after he told us he didn't know what was wrong, but whatever it was it didn't look good.

Then the real fear set in. John was old enough to be scared while Beverly and I were "out of our minds" terrified. The ophthalmologist examined our son and did not comfort us one bit. He said it looked like retinal blastoma (cancer of the eye) and got us into a specialist in the Detroit area a few days later.

Meanwhile, our whole life was put on hold. I couldn't work. I tried to reason with God. I argued with God, and then I even became very angry with God.

"How could You possibly allow this to happen?" I asked. "This boy has done nothing to hurt anyone, and this is how You treat Your people? I am not sure You are the God I want to serve."

The specialist told us he was not sure it was retinal blastoma but, to be on the safe side, he would have to remove that eye. I had, in the meantime, re-upped my faith in God and told the specialist I believed God could heal that eye. Without hesitation he looked me in the eyes and stated that there was no God known to man that could ever heal that eye and that it must come out.

We left that option open, but the next Sunday we asked the pastor to take time in the service to pray for healing in John's eye. He did, and God did not respond. We walked back to the pew with a three-year-old boy still blind in his right eye.

John soon experienced great pain as the eyeball began to swell up in the socket. Head pains were unbearable, and the doctor told us that John was experiencing greater pain than a woman delivering a baby with no anesthetic. All he did for the next few weeks was cry and moan. But we still had faith that as we prayed, God would be able to heal that eye.

The doctor was right. The great God that we serve did not heal that eye. At the age of thirty-nine John is still blind in his right eye. Where was God? Did He not answer our prayers?

In John 15:7 Jesus states:

> "If you remain in me and my words remain in you, ask whatever you wish, and it will be given you."

We did ask, and it seems that He just plain did not come through. In fact, we didn't see God answer that prayer until John was about sixteen years old. The answer was immediate. God had healed John, but we didn't see it until thirteen years later. God had healed John but not in the way we expected.

As John turned fifteen, our church had a softball team. We tried John in center field as he could run like the wind (unlike his dad) and he had perfect depth perception. We learned that it took both eyes to have depth perception, but John had it with one eye. He had been healed. Our son was not handicapped in any way. He even went on to be the soccer goalie on his college soccer team. Balls would come at him sixty to seventy miles per hour from ten feet away and John was able to stop them. He not only had quick, jerky moves, but he had perfect depth perception.

God had healed our son, but it took us thirteen years to realize it. Do you see what extra years give us? They allow us to have a greater understanding of some of the difficulties we go through. The extra years allow us to put all the pieces of the puzzle together to see that God is working behind the scenes and that He is, in fact, answering prayers.

It broke our hearts to see our three-year-old son crying and sobbing for more than a month. We even questioned why a loving God would allow an innocent, three-year-old child to experience such pain. I don't have any logical answers to that question; I just know God answers prayers and that my son was healed.

As the years go by and we enter the amazing golden years, all the tragedies in our life have come into a clearer focus. Some are lessons we must learn to live a fuller and richer life, and some are simply lessons, to give us a greater faith. I love the golden years and I love serving a God who is always with us, and I love serving the God who will never withdraw His love from us.

Study Questions:

1. Why do you suppose God doesn't always answer our prayers in the way we ask?

2. We see in John 16:24 another promise and a condition.
   a. What is the promise?
   b. What is the condition?
3. Why do you think Jesus said, "Your joy will be complete?"

Chapter 5

The Difficulties Got Worse

You've probably heard the saying "Cheer up. Things could be worse. So, I cheered up, and sure enough, things got worse." That is the way the year of prayer seemed to be shaping up. As if John's blindness and unbearable pain weren't enough, things got worse. Our oldest son was seven at the time and was a very active boy. He wanted to do everything. Brad loved peg-ball, flying Estes rockets, hiking, and just following me around whenever I was home. He also loved to run around the house in his underwear, and we were happy we were able to keep that much on him.

One day, as he was running around free from almost all clothing, Beverly and I noticed big bruises, at random, all over his body. I knew they weren't from a fall because they covered a lot of different areas of his body. Beverly and I were both puzzled because neither of us were parents who would ever beat our children.

We agreed to get him in to see a doctor the next day. That evening I was in Detroit having dinner with an account and excused myself to call home to find out what the doctor had said. The first words out of my wife's mouth were very unsettling. She asked if I was sitting down. Then she told me the doctor said that Brad was bleeding internally and that it looked like leukemia. That was devastating news. I was stunned. One son had just gone blind in one eye and now the other had leukemia.

I gathered my thoughts enough to ask what the doctor said the prognosis was. Beverly said, "Well, here is the bad news." I thought, "Bad news? Leukemia is the bad news. Now I want to know what we can do about it." But my wife unpacked the worst possible scenario and said, "If it is leukemia, the doctor said he only has a couple days to live." I ignored the words "If it is" and went right to the words "a couple days to live."

I was livid. God was messing with the family I loved so much. I made the kneejerk decision that I was done with ministry, with God, with church, and with everything else that reeked of anything spiritual. I was

The Difficulties Got Worse

done! I was not about to serve a God who was that mean and uncaring and possibly laughing at me.

I quickly excused myself from dinner and started the one-hour drive home. My car was full of screaming and yelling and crying all at the same time. I was out of my mind, and I was calling God names and using words that never should have come out of my mouth. I was angry and I didn't care if He was to strike me dead on the spot. I wanted Him to know the fullness of my wrath. If I died, at least He would know how I felt about the ministry and even about serving Him. I was done!

This rage went on for some time. About half an hour into the one-hour trip, I was worn out. I had reacted so violently that I had no energy left. All I could do was cry for the next few miles. Then as I began to calm down because of exhaustion, these thoughts started going through my mind. It was like God began to speak to me and I was able to listen.

The first thought was, "Can't I teach your son to play T-ball better than you?" I said, "Yes You can, God." Then, "Can't I teach your son to play soccer better than you?" Again, the answer was yes. Then, "Can't I teach your son to backpack better than you?" And the final answer was, "Yes, You can, God."

At that moment a very tender thought went through my mind. It was as if God said, "Then give him to Me." There was nothing I could do but obey. In my heart I raised Brad up in my hands and placed him into the loving hands of God. It was a sad moment and yet a very joyful moment at the same time. I knew that God loved Brad far more than I ever could and that He was able to protect my son from all the hurts and sorrows this world had to offer. I knew Brad would never be bullied or ever be sick again, and that comforted my sad and hurting heart. And I'm sure, however, that God could keep clothes on him any better than I could.

There is a story in the Bible about Abraham, a man whom God had chosen to begin the nation of Israel and bring righteousness into the world. God promised Abraham descendants as vast as the sand on the seashore even though he only had one son with his wife Sarah. Isaac was born to him when Abraham was one hundred years old. Abraham loved Isaac, and yet God asked him to do the impossible: to sacrifice his son.

What a questionable thing to do. First, God didn't believe in human sacrifices, and if this was Abraham's only legitimate son, how was God going to keep His promise to Abraham and give him descendants as numerous as the sand on the seashore?

To make a long story short (the entire story can be found in Genesis 22), Abraham was willing to go through with the request, but God stopped him at the last moment. In Genesis 22:12 God said,

> "Do not lay a hand on the boy—Do not do anything to him. Now I know that you fear God, because you have not withheld from me your son, your only son."

I sometimes equate my situation to that of Abraham's. God wanted to make sure that Abraham would trust Him and never allow anything in life to be put before Him, not even his only son, the son of a great promise. As we were praying about the ministry, was God testing me in a similar way? Was I in danger of putting someone or something ahead of God in my life? It didn't matter whether it was one of my sons, my daughter, or even my wife. Was I in danger of loving someone or something more than I loved God?

The following passage will help define this harsh message. Jesus was traveling with a large crowd following Him. Some wanted to be near Him because He spoke truth and logic and they wanted to become sincere disciples. Others wanted to follow Him for what He could do for them and for ways He could give them an advantage in life. Some simply wanted to be healed so they could get on with life without Him. Still others were His enemies and just wanted to put Him down.

With all this going on around Him, Jesus began to define the condition of discipleship. It is like He was deliberately trying to thin the crowd down and gather around Him only those who would desire to be true discipleship. I would guess the following verses helped Him define that goal.

> Luke 14:25–26: "Large crowds were traveling with Jesus, and turning to them He said, 'If anyone comes after me and does not hate his father and mother, his wife and his children, yes even his own life, he cannot be my disciple'".

Now that was blunt. From these verses we see that Jesus had no desire to hide the requirements of discipleship from the crowd or from me. He is not trying to soften the requirements and have a following of twelve thousand people by making everything sound easy and prosperous. It almost sounds like He is deliberately trying to thin the crowd and end up with a few sincere disciples. He is pushing those away who desire to follow Jesus for self-centered reasons. He is building a group of true followers who will be able to endure any hardships that will certainly come their way.

Jesus used the word "hate" in these verses to reveal to us how much greater our love for Him must be as compared to our love for family. He is not speaking against the fifth commandment, which tells us to honor our father and mother, but rather to esteem Him far more than our mother and father. Our love for Jesus is to be much greater than our love for anyone else, including ourselves, our children, and our spouse. Plus, when these verses were spoken, some of the followers had to reject their heritage of Judaism to follow Jesus. That meant they had to reject the teaching of their fathers and mothers, which meant shunning and separation.

Was God testing me to see if I had relationships that I was putting ahead of Him? Was He revealing to me that if I were going into the ministry, there would be some harsh trials ahead? Was He revealing to me that the only way I could survive the trials was to put my full allegiance and trust in Him? It seemed like a harsh lesson at the time, but it was a lesson I needed to learn.

As I am now in my seventies, I can look back over my life and see the lessons God was teaching me. They were lessons I had to learn if I was to become a pastor. These are truly the golden years. I can look back and see that all the trials and difficulties I went through were lessons and gifts from God.

To bring this story about Brad to a conclusion, we brought him home instead of admitting him to the hospital as the doctor suggested. We just wanted to spend as much time with him as possible. We took him off all medications, as they just seemed useless if he only had two days to live.

Two days later Brad started getting better. He was on an antibiotic that had sulfa in it, and we later became aware that he was allergic to sulfa. That antibiotic was killing him. Today, Brad is forty-two years old, married, and has two beautiful children. It was just another lesson we had to experience to go into the ministry. It was a harsh lesson at the time, but I am so grateful that I can look back now and thank God for the added quality of life I was given because of this lesson.

Study Questions:

1. What is one of the hardest trials you have had to go through in your life?
2. If you have been able to analyze that trial, what was God trying to help you understand and thus help you grow into a stronger disciple?
3. How did you feel when you were going through that trial?
    Toward God?
    Toward unanswered prayer?
    Toward a God who seemed to have detached Himself from your life?
4. Is there anything or anyone in your life that you are unwilling to give up in order to be a disciple of Jesus?

Chapter 6

The Trials Keep Coming

Before I went into the ministry, my work as an adidas salesman and later as a sales manager was a very prestigious profession. Adidas was the hottest new athletic shoe on the market, and to be associated with that product made me a high-profile person. I drove nice cars, traveled across the United States, and flew to Europe for business meetings.

But I did not share the prestige alone. My daughter Sha (long "a") also enjoyed the prestige, as I furnished adidas shoes at a minimal cost for her volleyball, basketball, and softball teams. Sha was proud of her dad and the position he held.

When we went into the ministry, it meant we would have to move from Williamston to Owosso, thirty miles away. Sha did not appreciate the move and she rebelled, especially since it meant moving to a different town as she entered her junior year in high school. When her new friends in Owosso asked her what her dad did, she would respond, "He used to be an adidas rep," and the word "minister" was never spoken.

She was not happy, and in hindsight I wonder if it was wise to move her at that time in her life. We could have stayed in Williamston where she was raised, as it would have only been a thirty-mile commute for me. It was a little unfair to pull her out of the class C school she had attended all her life and transfer her into a large class A school beginning her junior year. She had some wonderful lifetime friends in Williamston. But we did what we thought God was calling us to do, and she rebelled. During our year of prayer, she started the rebellion. She was not a terrible person; she just seemed very angry with us for the next two years.

We were a family of five, and to have one of the five be continually at odds and continually negative made the home just a little bit uncomfortable. The boys were young at the time, and that put them at a very obedient and pleasant age. They caused no trouble. But Sha, being a firstborn and a *little* strong-willed (like her dad), was very capable of stirring things up.

She was so upset she hardly spoke to us that year. In fairness to her, she had some very close friends in Williamston. She had gone to school there all her life and she felt like she would lose everything and start life over again from the ground up. The next six years (high school and college), Beverly and I prayed a lot for our daughter, and yet month after month, year after year, it seemed God was not answering.

As we have entered the amazing golden years, however, we have looked back over our life, and we realize that sometimes God answers prayers right away and sometimes He takes His sweet time. He took His own sweet time on this occasion, but we have come to realize He was just putting natural things in place so they would work out exactly as we prayed. That was what was happening.

We prayed and God began to put things in place behind the scenes. We prayed more and God put even more things in place to answer our prayers for Sha. We could not see what He was doing behind the scenes, but Beverly and I were amazed at how things changed after six years. One of our prayers was for Sha to find and marry a godly man.

God answered that prayer. Beverly was having a Bible study with Cherie, whose husband, John, was from California. As she asked for prayer for Sha, Cherie told about one of her husband's best friends from California who was now living in Bend, Oregon. He was a single, very godly man and had asked Cherie to find him a wife.

Cherie communicated to Dave that she had found him his future wife. Dave flew to Michigan to meet Sha. She then flew to Bend, Oregon, for a week to experience Dave's lifestyle. She came back engaged and was married two months later. It was amazing. For six years we prayed for our daughter, and within four months from my wife's prayer request, Sha was married to a very godly and wonderful husband.

Then, as a footnote to that, Sha called us two years after her wedding and asked us to pray about the ministry. I was just a little set back and asked her which way she wanted us to pray, and she said, "I think God is calling Dave into the ministry." Now there is a turn of events. She rebelled when we went into the ministry, and then she was willing to become a pastor's wife. What an amazing God we serve. He does have a sense of humor.

In the amazing golden years, we can look back and see that at times God answers prayers right away and sometimes He takes His time, but He always answers if we pray according to His will. Jesus said in John 16:24:

> "Until now you have not asked for anything in my name. Ask and you will receive, and your joy will be complete."

Now we have two options to deal with concerning this verse. Either Jesus is a liar (and I don't want to stand next to you in a thunderstorm if that is your choice) or He will answer our prayers if we pray according to His will. Sometimes He answers right away, sometimes He takes His time, and then sometimes He answers in ways we don't even recognize. But He always answers, and that is a fact. I just love these amazing golden years because we can now look back over life and see the miracles God has worked and the beautiful blessings He has poured into our lives.

Yet that year of prayer about going into the ministry was still not over. John had gone blind in one of his eyes, we were told Brad had leukemia and only had two days to live, and we experienced our daughter, Sha, rebel and stir up the family. As if that were not enough, we were told that my wife, Beverly, might have breast cancer. She had a mammogram and a lump showed up. It was scary to hear the words "cancer" and "Beverly" show up in the same sentence.

At first, I wasn't really concerned; in fact, I was a little angry. Beverly and I were both convinced that the lab results were not my wife's but had gotten mixed up with another woman's. We were angry that the staff at the hospital was revealing their incompetence. Why didn't they double-check whose name was on those x-rays?

I called the hospital and argued with them. "Why would you scare our family when you should be calling another family?" I'm not sure how I came to that conclusion, but I felt sure I was right beyond a reasonable shadow of doubt. I simply would not accept the diagnosis. Down deep I think I simply refused to accept it.

The lab results turned out to be hers, and I, once again, began to question God as to why He was allowing all this to happen, especially since we were committing the rest of our lives to His ministry and to doing Kingdom work. This was just another mountain to scale during our year of prayer.

Then we began to entertain the thought that maybe God was shutting the door on our ministry venture. Maybe He was telling us that going into the ministry was not on His radar screen and we really should reconsider. Or was the Evil One trying to discourage us from making such a life-changing option? All sorts of questions began to enter our minds.

As we have matured into the golden years, we realized God was just preparing us for the ministry and seeing how committed we really were. Would we be able to stand up to some of the mountains we would have to face in the ministry? Would our faith in Him be strong enough to trust Him in some difficult situations? Was our family strong enough to stay together when troubles come to tear it apart?

A needle biopsy was done, and the lump was benign. Whether God was testing us or the Evil One was trying to discourage us, I'm not sure. I just wish sometimes God would speak audibly to me. Yet it always seems that the Holy Spirit puts thoughts in my mind that I cannot set aside. The third person in the Trinity, God's spokesman, does instruct me with thoughts that are too powerful to overlook. Beverly did not have cancer. Praise the Lord!

Then the scariest day of all came upon us. It was "decision day." We had prayed for one year, excited about the possibility of going into the ministry and even asking our friends to pray for us as we shared our excitement. Three hundred sixty-five days had finally passed, and the praying and talking and sharing of our excitement had come to an end. It was time to say, "Yes, God has called us into the ministry" or "No, He has not."

It was decision time, and I still didn't feel I had gotten a clear answer one way or the other. Reality set in during the first few hours of decision day. Did I really want to give up the dream job I had and set aside the large income I was making? What was I thinking? Was I going through a midlife crisis? Should I just go out and buy a Corvette to satisfy my desire to change? Was I losing my mind? Was I putting my family in jeopardy? Was I even considering my family? What if this new career didn't work out? What if I failed?

I had committed to make the decision on this date. Now I didn't know if I could make that decision. It was Sunday morning, and as soon as I arrived at church, my pastor asked what the decision was. He had been praying for me and was just as excited as I was.

I thought for a moment, maybe five seconds, and without any hesitation said, "Ministry." I had worried about it all morning, trying to second-guess myself, trying to make some semblance of logic out of it. But when it came right down to it, God was calling me into the ministry, and whether it was the logical decision or not, I was excited, and I had to do it. I knew that was the answer, because that was all I could dream about.

Adidas had been put on a back burner during that year. I had lost interest in that profession.

I never heard an audible answer from God saying, "Yes, I want you to go into the ministry." But in hindsight, I knew that was the answer because every day of that year of prayer, my heart got more and more excited about the new profession. Then, when I made the change, I came to realize it was the most gratifying career I could possibly be a part of.

STUDY QUESTIONS:

1. Name a time in your life when you had to make a life-changing decision without hearing a definite direction from God.
2. Why do you feel God doesn't always give us a clear direction and say, "This is the way"?
3. Look up John 16:24. Why did Jesus add the word joy to this verse. How does the word "joy" enter into the formula of God's answer?
4. What do you think it means to ask in Jesus's name?

Chapter 7

The Failed Cottage Plan

About the time we were considering going into the ministry, I had a personal goal of owning a cottage on a beautiful lake in northern Michigan. We could afford one, and it seemed like a wonderful plan for my young family. But because of the condition of the church we chose to go to, I realized that plan was not going to happen. The church had a very small congregation, was heavily indebted, and the people didn't have a lot of extra money lying around. The building had great potential, as it was new. It was seventeen thousand square feet but not finished on the interior. Only twenty percent of the church was partially finished. The other two-thirds were walls with studs showing and a lot of dust, and it was used as a large storage area.

There were only fourteen people left in the church when we came, as it had gone through some difficult times. They were very godly and loving people and very accepting of an adidas salesman turned minister. But the church was in such bad financial shape that they were unable to pay me for the first four months I was there. No cottage in northern Michigan in my near future.

I was okay with that and let the cottage dream fade because of my joy in becoming a pastor. It was just something I had to sacrifice in order to do God's will in my life. I figured that since we had some amazing vacations in my previous profession, I would be happy to take inexpensive vacations now.

But my Lord had other plans for us, and He put two different things in place to make up for the personal cottage we desired. First, because we were required to go to church camp during the summer, we bought a pop-up camper. That camper also served as our cabin on the lake for the next twelve years. We camped on some of the most beautiful lakes in northern Michigan during that time.

OUR POP-UP CAMPER

The Failed Cottage Plan

The boys were five and seven at the time, and a perfect age to take camping. Sha was sixteen, and she opted out of some of our trips, but we had even more fun when she was able to come along. We had bonfires in the morning and evening. We cooked s'mores and hiked many trails. Even though the camper was only three years old, I had a lot of fun remodeling the inside a little. I took out one bed that was not needed and installed five drawers, giving each family member a drawer instead of tripping over five suitcases every time we moved.

I added a gas/electric refrigerator, which replaced the icebox. We had a lot of fun in that camper and used it until the boys started college. Every spring I would wax the camper to remove the yearly discoloration on the paint. That camper looked brand-new for years. Initially it was a much less expensive way of owning a place on the lake.

I was okay with giving up the cottage on the lake because God had provided an alternative. Plus, the close quarters with my family provided Beverly and me with some beautiful memories. But then Sha got married and the boys went off to college. When that happened, the pop-up camper lost some of its excitement. Without the children around, camping wasn't quite as much fun.

Once again, we revisited the dream of a cottage. But that dream was even further from a possibility because we were experiencing the poorest years of our life. The church was willing to pay us as much as they could afford. They were very gracious and generous to us. But, instead of buying new cars, we were buying used cars with more than one hundred thousand miles on them. Plus, it seemed we were always praying for money to purchase the bare necessities of life.

Then God put His second plan in place to bless our lives. Over the next ten years, He provided us with five different cottages. Three of them were even on lakes in northern Michigan. They were cottages different friends owned, and they were free to us. As I look back on that blessing, Mark 10:28–30 comes to mind. The disciples were concerned because they left everything to follow Jesus.

> "Peter said to him, 'We have left everything to follow you!' 'I tell you the truth,' Jesus replied, 'no one who has left home or brothers or sisters or mother or father or children or fields for me and the gospel will fail to receive a hundred times as much in this present age [homes, brothers, sisters, mothers, children and fields—and

The Failed Cottage Plan

with them, persecutions] and in the age to come, eternal life.'"

THIS IS ONE OF THE LOG CABIN COTTAGES WE USED ON LAKE SUPERIOR.

THE INTERIOR OF THE CABIN WAS RUSTIC AND BEAUTIFUL.

It was an amazing blessing to us because, unlike owning a cottage, we never had to mow a lawn, repair the cottage, replace broken appliances, or pay for fire insurance. We never had to repaint the bedroom, purchase new carpet, or replace worn-out furniture. We never had to pay taxes or association fees. These five cottages were truly a blessing from God. It was the best possible way to go to a cottage. It was free!

I used two of the cottages to get away and write part of my master's thesis. Beverly and I used one to spend part of our sabbatical in. We used them for vacations, and I even used one to get away to spend a day in prayer. Because we were willing to give up our cottage dream to go into the ministry, God blessed us with a far greater plan.

It was interesting how He provided each one. The most unique story was a cottage we were given on Lake Superior. It was a new log cabin built by the Amish. I don't think the water temperature ever gets above forty degrees in the summer on Lake Superior, but we spent many restful weeks up there. It was because of another embarrassing moment in my life that we were offered that cabin.

I was visiting a couple in rural Owosso. The family had been very successful farmers but had retired by that time. They lived in an older farmhouse that had a dangerous back entry. I went into the back room one day and climbed the steps to enter the dining room. At the top step, I fell flat on my face into the dining room. The steps were uneven in height, and I learned as a builder that if one step is even ¾ of an inch different in height, it can cause one to trip. I tripped and the couple rushed to the phone to call 911.

I was okay, but to cover my embarrassment, I explained the problem and warned them that they could fall and hurt themselves because of the difference in the height of each step. Even though this had never happened to them in ten years, I was just trying to make an excuse to cover my own clumsiness.

Because of the fall, I offered to build them new steps where each step would be the same height. They graciously agreed that it would probably be a good idea and told me to go ahead. When finished, they were very pleased and thought the new steps were beautiful. They thought the rail on one side was a wonderful new safety feature.

To thank me they gave me the keys to their new log cabin on Lake Superior. The only two stipulations were that I had to check with their schedule to make sure we didn't all show up at the same time, plus we couldn't use it during snowmobile season. God provided us the use of a cottage with no upkeep, no taxes, and no worries. Isn't that just like God?

Another cottage was a very large log cabin on Lake Charlevoix. It came with a ski boat we could use. The cabin was large enough to have all three of our children, their spouses, and two grandchildren come and visit. We used it one year for a family vacation.

The owner was a very wealthy man who, at one time, owned 120 newspapers across the United States. I had befriended him in a charitable organization we both belonged to, and then when I went into the ministry, I suggested we do a Bible study together. He was willing.

John seemed to be grateful for the interest I took in his spiritual life, and his beautiful cottage became our beautiful cottage. We boated, water-skied, and just had a wonderful time using our log cabin on beautiful Lake Charlevoix.

We were blessed with five cottages. Could life get any better than that? I will have to admit, however, that I failed to recognize the total blessing until the beginning of my golden years. I knew it was a blessing but failed to equate our desire to own a cabin with God's willingness to give us one. I love being seventy-three.

The Failed Cottage Plan

It allows me to see all the blessings God has poured into my life.

The scriptures, however, state that we will receive one hundred times as many cottages as we gave up in our dream, so I am still waiting for ninety-five more. Maybe they will be on the French Riviera or some South Seas island.

Study Questions:

1. What were (are) you willing to give up to become a faithful Christ follower (drugs, some worldly dream, pride, forgiveness, relationships, career)?
2. What blessings have you experienced from God as a result of giving them up (health, better relationships, more than you could dream, complete joy)?
3. What is God asking you to give up that you are afraid to let go of?

Chapter 8

The Blessings My Family Gave Me

As you read chapter one, you may have noticed that I felt embarrassed about my family because of how poor I perceived we were. We lived in a cement-block house with a cement floor. The house was more like a garage than a house. In fact, the first part of the house we lived in was built as a future garage. As the family expanded, an addition was added to that section, but the proposed garage remained a central part of the house. I felt we lived just a few inches above the worms.

Our cement-block house before the addition.

We tried to paint the blocks on the outside with a new miracle paint they came out with back in the 1950s, but within two years, it was fading and peeling off. Our house was then a rose color, a faded rose color, and a cement-block color. It was not real attractive. I was embarrassed to tell people where we lived, and I don't ever remember inviting any friends over from school. My only friends were neighbors who came over to play, and it was impossible to hide the looks of our home from them.

The interior of the house was always messy, as eight people lived in a small area and Mom was always busy working, cooking, doing the laundry, and caring for our family. My older brother and I shared an attic bedroom upstairs. The walls were the roof rafters, and if we wanted to walk standing up, we had to walk down the very center of the room. Even then we had to bend over a little.

I can remember Dad visiting our bedroom maybe once a year and losing control of his emotions. The room was so messy and so dusty that Dad would go into a rage. It was a little scary. He never beat us or hit us, but he just lost control. The outcome of those visits were ultimatums.

He did come back, but it was usually a year later, and the room was as messy as before, if not worse. That would ignite the rage all over again. My Dad was not a monster; he just expected some semblance of orderliness. I guess it came from his army background. Again, with the house that messy, I never invited school friends into our home, and if the neighbor kids came over, I would never consider inviting them upstairs to my bedroom.

And then there were the clothes we wore. They were hand-me-downs and always showed wear. If we wanted them to be ironed, we had to iron them ourselves, as Mom was busy cooking for eight hungry people. She also drove a small school bus twice a day. As I entered junior high, I began buying a lot of my own clothes with money I earned from mowing lawns and bailing hay. I often wondered how many of my classmates had to buy their own clothes.

I didn't begin to realize until later how much pride I had in me. In later years, as I have shared some of my embarrassing moments with my classmates, they have responded, "We never thought you were any poorer than we were." With that statement from my friends, I am beginning to realize how prideful I was and still am.

The Blessings My Family Gave Me

I always looked up to my cousin Beth. She is my age, and we used to have so much fun together. Beth was an only child, and it seemed like she had everything. Her family had nice cars, owned a beautiful home in the suburbs, and had a lawn that was so perfect my dad told us it would be best if we didn't walk on it. Beth had everything, and to me she had a perfect life.

Then one day, in my later years, we got together with Beth and she began to share with me the life she really had. She said she always loved to come to visit us because we were a family. We had brothers and sisters to play with while she had none. There was always a lot of laughter in our family and she experienced mostly sadness growing up.

We had a mother and father who loved each other (most of the time) while her mother and father divorced, remarried, and then divorced again. That was the cause of a lot of yelling and screaming while our home was mostly peaceful (if we could just keep Dad from going upstairs). My cousin Beth really admired our family even though she seemed to have everything we didn't have.

Beth has helped me look back over my life and begin to add up the many blessings we had as a family. Yes, I was embarrassed, yet we were given far more than most families. First, Mom and Dad were very hard workers. They taught us if we wanted anything, we had to work for it. All my brothers and sisters picked up on that lesson, and each one has a good work ethic. My ironing skills even gave me an opportunity to earn money in college as none of my friends knew what an iron was.

Mom and Dad raised us in church. In fact, we went to church four times on Sunday (Sunday school, church, teens at night, and then evening service). They raised us in a moral atmosphere and put us in proximity with other church-going children. I really enjoyed our social life in that atmosphere, possibly more than the spiritual.

However, at the age of thirty-one, when I became a dissatisfied with my gain of earthly goods, I knew what I had to do because of my spiritual background. I knew what decision I had to make to discover a life that would never disappoint me and never let me down. If I never had godly parents and that spiritual background, I don't know what direction my life would have taken. I am so thankful I was raised in a church. The Bible tells us to:

> "Train a child in the way he should go,
> and when he is old he will not turn from
> it." Proverbs 22:6

The Blessings My Family Gave Me

I will have to admit that I departed from Christian teaching for fourteen years, but when I needed to go in a positive direction, I knew where to go. Maybe we didn't have a lot, but I am so thankful that my parents gave me the spiritual roots so I could find my way. I would suggest that you never underestimate the positive direction a spiritual upbringing will have on your children.

And there are so many more things Lorren and Marie Emerson gave to me. My Grandpa Emerson lived on a remote farm in northern Michigan. It was 160 acres cut out of a national forest, and it was beautiful. Being around five brothers and sisters at home, I loved getting away and visiting my grandpa all by myself.

One day my Dad drove me up there to drop me off, and Grandpa was telling him some of the things he wanted to get done that week. I will never forget my Dad saying that I would be a great help because I could do just about anything. Dad was bragging about me within my hearing, and I'm sure I stood just a little taller that day. What a blessing it was to hear my Dad tell his Dad how special I was.

I may have perceived that we were poor, but I was given many advantages that others only dreamed about receiving. Another thing that blessed me was that Dad attended every one of my football games. In fact, here is a picture of Dad that was in my senior yearbook.

PICTURE OF DAD IN MY YEARBOOK

I loved football but didn't have a great body for the game. I was six feet tall and weighed less than 150 pounds. I wasn't fast and had small hands, so I played an interior line position on offense and an outside linebacker on defense. On two separate occasions I got hurt.

The first time I got hit hard in the head, so I took myself out of the game. I sat on the bench for less than a minute and my Dad tapped me on the shoulder to see

The Blessings My Family Gave Me

if I was okay. At the time it embarrassed me, but later it made me realize how concerned he was for me. In truth I think it was Mom telling him to get his butt down there to see what was wrong with me.

The second injury was a sprained ankle. When you are young and you sprain your ankle for the first time, the pain is unbearable. They took me off the field on a stretcher, and as soon as we got to the sideline, there was my Dad. He held my head up a little as they examined my ankle.

In hindsight I was embarrassed about my family. Yet how many boys don't even have a father, and of those who do, how many have a father who never shows up to a game? I was blessed with things beyond the material realm. I was blessed with the thing that matters most: a loving and caring family. I just wished that I had honored them more during my teen years. That is the wisdom the golden years provide.

One of the things that I thought was quite normal was something else my Dad blessed me with. We lived in a rural area, but within one mile, there were enough kids to form a softball team. We would get together during the summer and play "workup" in our front yard. The yard was narrow, and a lot of the outfield was across the road, over a deep ditch, and out in the field.

Dad was not an athlete and I don't think he ever played softball, but he got the idea of forming a neighborhood softball team. He called us the Base Burners and started searching for other teams we could play. He also set up a softball diamond in an open field with a backstop made of chicken wire. For four summers we played softball at Base Burners Stadium.

Dad was very proud of the Base Burners. I have no idea how many games we won or lost; I just remember all the fun we had. I do remember how proud Dad was of one game we won. It was against a Boy Scouts troop in town. Dad got a kick out of beating them because we had girls playing first base, second base, and third base. He bragged about that for the rest of the summer. The Boy Scouts were not very happy getting beaten by the Base Burners.

As I look back over those years, I was given a big advantage over many children. Maybe we were a little poor, but I was raised in a solid family with parents who loved us and with a father who bragged about us and was always involved in our activities. I had what many children wanted. In hindsight I had a wonderful childhood. This is what makes the golden years amazing.

Study Questions:

1. Sometimes (often) our parents do things that embarrass us. Name a few things, however, your parents did to help you and make you feel safe. How grateful are you?
2. Name some positive lessons your family taught you to help you mature.
3. If your family added negative things to your life, how has God turned those negative things around, resulting in positive lessons?

Chapter 9

A More Recent Lesson

As I mentioned in the introduction, many of the difficult times I have endured were lessons God was trying to teach me. It happens because I have no trouble seeing the shortcomings in others but often have trouble seeing and admitting my own. That is when Jesus takes me through a situation and reveals a weakness I need to work on.

Recently I was taught another area in my life that needed that kind of attention. I will admit, when a situation arises that irritates me, I can become very angry, and anger is not a mood that lends itself to good Christian actions. Anger is more apt to chase people away from Jesus than draw them closer.

My wife and I were in Grand Rapids attending a meeting. Grand Rapids and its surrounding suburbs have a population of nearly four hundred thousand people. That is a big city compared to Owosso, where

A More Recent Lesson

I live. We have around seventeen thousand people, and the pace is just a little bit slower than Grand Rapids.

Our son, Brad, and his family live in the Grand Rapids area, so we planned to have lunch with them. We chose one of our favorite restaurants. It is an out-of-the way deli that only the locals are aware of. It is not fancy, but very busy, and does not have nearly enough parking spaces to accommodate the lunch traffic that usually shows up.

Beverly and I were just a little late, so we were both on edge when we discovered there were no parking spaces within two blocks of the place. There was nothing available in the front, the tiny parking lot in the back was full, and the side street had cars parked on both sides for two blocks.

We drove down the side street and then back toward the restaurant hoping and praying a spot would become available. Just as we approached the parking lot in back, we saw a man come out of the back door and get in his car. We were so excited and began to thank God for hearing our prayers.

I stopped on the side street so as not to clog up the small parking lot and put my right blinker on to show everyone that was my spot and I was just waiting for the man to pull out. Not a good plan. As soon as his car began to back up, a man came around the corner, saw a space, and turned into the parking lot, taking *my space*!

Now to say that did not sit well with me is putting it mildly. The whites in my eyes turned red, and I would guess I looked a little scary for a moment. I was so upset that I pulled my car up on the sidewalk and parked there. It was a very tense moment and it became even more tense as my wife ("By-the-rules Beverly") began to lecture me how improper that was. She even suggested our car might be towed or that we might end up spending time in jail.

I hardly heard her because my focus was to go into the restaurant and stand in line behind the "Grand Rapids Grabber" and decide then and there how to get even. We did stand in line right behind him and I did begin to determine my next step.

Realizing our son and his family were already there, Beverly asked if it would be okay if she went and sat with them while I ordered. I knew what she wanted from the menu, so I told her to go ahead. Then she asked me a question that seemed so strange coming from her and something she had never asked me before. She asked, "There isn't going to be a fistfight here, is there?"

That was an odd question because she knew I was not a violent man, plus she knew I had never hit a man in the face with my fist. But as she asked it, I know it bothered the Grand Rapids Grabber because he turned slightly and looked over his shoulder to measure me up and to see what he had to contend with. He heard Beverly's question and it concerned him just a little.

Beverly went and sat down with our son and his family while I patiently schemed what my next "get-even move" might be. As I considered it, the following thought passed through my mind. I wondered what it would feel like if I were to put my hand on the back of his neck and *slam* his face down on the counter, giving him a bloody nose and possibly knocking a couple of his teeth out. But I want you to understand that I am not a violent man.

The Grand Rapids Grabber gave his order to the waitress, and she asked what his name was so the sandwich could be delivered when ready. He said his name was Al. Then she asked him if he was there alone and he looked back over his shoulder with a sad look on his face and said, "Yes." I thought, "Serves you right for what you did. You are all alone, and I am here with three generations of the Emerson family. Poor, poor man."

Al went and sat down, and I placed my order and went and sat down with my family. My wife had enlightened our son as to what had happened and that I might be in a slightly tense mood. To help me he said, "Dad, people are more aggressive in the city." That just added to my anger because I needed sympathy, not insight.

After lunch I drove home still pondering how evil Al was and what I should have done to get even. The Grand Rapids Grabber was not a nice person, and I told him that repeatedly. Of course, he was not there to listen to me, and that bothered me even more.

I realized I wasn't going to sleep that night unless I was able to let go of my anger. So, I did something I should have done while walking in the back door of the restaurant. I began to pray and asked God to forgive me for my self-centered anger. Then I asked God to help me forgive Al. I didn't want to pray that prayer and am not sure how sincere I was, but I knew that was the only way to get some sleep.

The Lord God was able to lead me and direct me through scripture I had read over the past several days. The verses were:

> Ephesians 5:15–16 "Be very careful then how you live—not as unwise but as wise, making the most of every opportunity, because the days are evil."

A More Recent Lesson

Making the most of every opportunity? The Grand Rapids Grabber gave me the opportunity to do something good or to do a good deed to someone who had hurt me. He gave me the opportunity to reveal the joy in my life instead of the anger.

An opportunity like that doesn't come along every day, and I am commanded to make it into something very positive. Had I done that, even if I would never have mentioned the name of Jesus, that man would have recognized me as a very kind person, which is just the opposite of how I came across. It may have even given me the chance to start up a new friendship. I can only imagine how God could have used that situation to bring glory to Himself.

The next two verses followed, and they are:

> Ephesians 5:17–18 "Therefore do not be foolish, but understand what the Lord's will is. Do not get drunk on wine, which leads to debauchery [wildness]. Instead be filled with the Spirit."

The word "Spirit" is spelled with a capital "S," which refers to the Holy Spirit. That is a gift from God to every Christian who has made Jesus the Lord of his or her life. God's Spirit dwells within each of us. That Spirit brings us God's wisdom from above. Therefore, at every second of every day, I have access to the wisdom of God to resolve any situation I might find myself in.

That evening, in order to calm down, I began to pray, "Lord, I need You now. If You want me to make the most of every opportunity, then I need to hear from You. What could I have done for Al that would have brought glory to You and eased my tension?"

That is a prayer I should have prayed before I got in line behind Al. According to the answers that started to come, I missed out on a great opportunity to bring glory to God and peace to my own heart. Plus, I realized I will never be able to redo that encounter and replay my role in order to have a different outcome.

Because of that prayer, God began to help me see things from Al's point of view. It is very likely that he was in such a hurry that he may never have seen my car sitting there with my blinker on. I also began to look at his day and the possible things he went through before he stole my parking space. Perhaps he was just overlooked for a promotion he had worked hard for and rightly deserved. Maybe he had just received unwanted divorce papers from his wife. Perhaps he had just received news that one of his children was in jail because of unlawful distribution of drugs or in the hospital because of a drug overdose. The Spirit revealed to me that I was seeing everything from my self-centered perspective and not from his.

Then thoughts continued to come. If Al knew I was upset with him from the "fistfight" comment, how would he have responded if I had offered to pay for his meal? He would likely have rejected the idea, but an offer like that could have melted his heart or at least put his heart at ease.

I also began to wonder what he would have said if I had told him I would love to have lunch with him since he was all alone. That would have, again, possibly been too much but maybe been very inviting had he just gone through some trauma. A listening ear may have been inviting.

Any of those scenarios may have been possible had I prayed for the leading and wisdom of the Holy Spirit before I ever got in line behind Al. Now they are all afterthoughts. I will say that I slept well that night. I was able to stop talking to Al and started being blessed by the Holy Spirit, who dwells within me.

The next Bible verses that came to me are verses I can still act on. They are verses that direct my future in similar situations.

> Ephesians 5:19b–20: "Sing and make music in your heart to the Lord, always giving thanks to God the Father for everything, in the name of our Lord Jesus Christ."

Giving thanks to God for everything? I can still do that.

Even though the Grand Rapids Grabber gave me a moment of grief, which quickly turned to anger, I can give thanks to God for the lesson I was able to take away from that encounter. It gave me a very clear picture of what my anger really looks like and how it can destroy me and everyone around me. One of my children told me how one of my fits of rage really scared him at the age of eight, even though it was directed at a cat and not at him. To think that I put that kind of fear into the heart of one of my children really breaks my heart.

I can give thanks to God when I realize how different the outcome might have been had I sent up a quick S.O.S. to God as I walked into that restaurant. I know from other situations that He would have quickly responded and guided me into a whole different response toward Al.

Plus, I can give thanks to God for the lesson I learned. Because of that insight I hope never again to be so angry I would want to slam a man's face on a countertop (even though I am not a violent man). That anger brought me a feeling of power, but it was such a negative power that it brought me no pleasure. It only brought me a feeling of depression.

STUDY QUESTIONS:

1. Explain a situation in your life when your response toward someone was not as positive as it could have been.
2. How could you have responded differently?
3. How could God have used your different response to bring Him glory?
4. How could God have used your different response to bring *joy* into your life?

Chapter 10

House Fire

It was the late 1950s, and men were just beginning to take up the manly art of using charcoal to grill Sunday meals. Dad seemed to be very proud of his exceptional culinary skills and offered to prepare the Sunday dinner on Mother's Day. Preparation to him meant putting the hamburgers on the grill, turning them over when they started to burn, then taking them in the house and announcing, "Dinner is ready." I'm not sure where the rest of the food came from, but it was on the table when Dad arrived.

It was a delicious meal, as Dad had put some pieces of wood on the charcoal to give the hamburgers a smoky flavor. Little did he realize that the wood sent sparks into the wood box near the house, and when the wood box caught fire, the house caught fire.

After dinner my brother and I went across the road to play football in the neighbor's front yard while Dad took a nap after laboring over a hot grill. We were about half an hour into the game when I looked across the road and noticed a lot of smoke coming from the back of our house.

My mind intermittently went into slow motion mode as I chuckled and said, "Look, something is burning ... Oh my, our house is on fire!" I raced across the road and into the house just in time for Dad to hand me the phone, telling me to give the fire department our address. As I talked to them, I had to keep getting lower and lower to the floor as the heavy black smoke grew thicker and thicker.

We lived in a small town and the fire department was made up of volunteers. It was a beautiful Sunday afternoon and Mother's Day, and it seemed to take forever for one of the volunteers to arrive at the fire barn and take my call to get the address of the fire. Then it took time for the rest of the volunteers to get there and get the trucks rolling.

I finally heard the trucks coming down the road with sirens blaring, and to help them find the right house, I stood out in the middle of the road and waved them in. I think I was afraid they might miss the billowing black smoke that could be seen for miles and drive right by our house.

As they started to put the fire out, I looked out on the road, and car after car drove by slowly, just gawking at our burning home. It seemed like two or three heads were hanging out the windows as the cars drove by, turned around at the closest driveway, and then drove back with two or three heads hanging out the windows on the other side of the car. Our house was burning, and people were just driving by, enjoying a little Sunday afternoon entertainment.

They all seemed to be enjoying their Sunday drive, watching a house burn that eight people called home. I wanted to go out by the road and tell them all to just go home. It was a long afternoon, and by nightfall we had no place to live. We had no clean clothes to wear, as everything smelled of that heavy, black smoke, and we had no place to sleep. I wondered where God was in all of it. Then He began to show His face.

The neighbors offered to let us stay in their basement until we could make other arrangements. So, we dragged all our smoky mattresses over to their house. The next day Dad drove to an Army PX store in Detroit and bought a 16'x16' army tent and pitched it in our backyard. Guess where we spent the rest of our summer.

House Fire

TENT CITY. THE TENT TO THE RIGHT WAS OUR BEDROOM AND THE ONE BEHIND US WAS THE LIVING ROOM.

Our family of eight camped out in the backyard for four months, and that made it even more embarrassing. Why couldn't we rent a house like a normal family would have done? Dad built an outhouse behind the barn, which was normal for him, as that was what he had when he grew up. But in the late 1950s everyone had indoor plumbing except the Emerson family. He also built a small lean-to behind the tent where we could bathe with a bucket of cold water.

I am sure people drove by and said to themselves, "That poor Emerson family. Look at how they have to live." I am sure the neighbors thought we were lowering their property value, as Tent City was our new mailing address.

But God was in it all. The church took up a special offering to help us out. Some ladies in the community went store to store asking for all kinds of donations, from clothing to toiletries and even food. I realized, however, there is a lot more dignity in helping others get back on their feet than personally needing help.

Looking back on that summer, it was the healthiest one our family of eight ever experienced. No one got sick, even though we spent days outside in the rain. I can even remember a couple of times wearing our wet clothes until they dried out on our bodies. It was quite an experience.

Dad was clever enough to provide everything we needed to survive. In fact, he and Mom made it a little fun. I'll never forget what happened in late August, a few days after we moved back into what seemed like a brand-new home. The place seemed like a castle with a lot of extra room even though it was only 1,236 square feet with an attic that had two bedrooms. Still, after living in a 256-square-foot 16'x16' army tent, our home seemed like a palace.

House Fire

The home was beautiful. The repaired parts were of a higher quality than the original parts, plus the areas that had not been completed before the fire were totally done. The kitchen cabinets went from a roughly constructed painted pine to beautiful custom cabinets made of redwood plywood.

The back porch that housed the washer and dryer was completely torn down and a new porch was added, which included a half bath. That half bath was a little cold in the winter, but sometimes cold just didn't matter when there was a waiting line for the full bathroom. The remodeled house became a real luxury after living in tent city for four months.

Then something special happened after we moved back into the house. I will never forget the conversation between Mom and Dad. We had been in the house less than a week, and Dad said, "Marie, I have a vacation coming yet this summer." Mom inquired, "Okay, Lorren, what would you like to do?" I was thinking we would go visit Grandpa Emerson in northern Michigan (my favorite choice) or Grandma Brown in Ypsilanti. But instead Dad said, "Let's go camping." Mom agreed, and within a couple days we were packed and on the road. That was the beginning of many happy camping vacations. What a blessing.

But on that first outing, after setting up and tearing down that heavy army tent three times in one week, Mom gently persuaded Dad to build a camper. The next spring plans were drawn up and construction got underway. It was twelve feet long and slept eight. It had an aisle down the middle with a closet on the end that held all our clothes. It also had a kitchen cabinet on the outside of the camper under the awning. In my mind that camper was a masterpiece. My dad was a genius. And to think those camping vacations may never have happened had our house not burned on Mother's Day.

THIS IS THE HOMEMADE CAMPER DAD MADE. MOM AND DAD WERE CAMPING HERE WITH ANOTHER FAMILY. LOOK WHO HAD TO DO THE DISHES.

God is so good! At the time, the fire was a tragedy. I can remember thinking, "Where are we going to live? What are we going to eat, as all our food is ruined? What clothes will we wear?" But then God tells us:

> "Therefore I tell you, do not worry about your life, what you will eat or drink: or about your body, what you will wear. Is not life more important than clothes? Look at the birds of the air; they do not sow or reap or stow away in barns, and yet your heavenly Father feeds them. Are you not more valuable than they?
> Matthew 6:25-26

And God did feed us and clothe us!

As I grow older, I realize how God has blessed our lives. He was able to take the tragedy of our house burning and turn it into a beautiful, newly remodeled home. He was able to show us that the community did care for us as it stepped in to provide us with a place to stay, new clothes, and food. But it also introduced us to a new and exciting way to go on vacation. In fact, that first camping trip was the first vacation I can remember our family ever taking.

God was able to reveal that the embarrassment of tent city became a healthy and fun summer. We even spent a lot of time driving to the lake to go swimming. Plus, that fire introduced us to the world of camping, and because of that, Beverly and I have become the owners of three separate campers during our marriage. We have experienced many happy camping experiences with our own family.

Study Questions:

1. Consider a tragedy that happened in your family. How did God make something good come out of it?
2. Each family has at least one parent who is gifted in something special. As you consider your tragedy, how did that giftedness reveal itself?

Chapter 11

Why I Was Never Pastor of a Big Church

I WENT INTO THE MINISTRY WHEN I was thirty-nine years old with only one year of ministry classes under my belt, so I was given a small church. It was a troubled church with only fourteen people worshiping there at the time. I was excited because the structure was seventeen thousand square feet and new. Most of it was unfinished on the inside, but my background in construction helped me see the potential. The location was prime, and the remaining congregation was a godly group of people.

I went at ministry with great energy and enthusiasm, promising that we would be worshiping one hundred strong by the end of the first year. Success in my previous career gave me the confidence to make such a claim, but it didn't happen. Growth was strong, and in the next few years we won several awards for both physical and spiritual growth. However, it took around six years before we reached one hundred people at our Sunday morning worship service.

We went through seven building programs over the next twenty years to complete the building and make it ready for the potential growth. Construction included a completed Sunday school wing and then a completed sanctuary. A new front parking lot helped traffic see there were people actively worshiping at the church. Mr. Cram, one of the older members, asked why we had to turn the beautiful front lawn into a parking lot. I told him that when they built the church, they made a mistake and put the front door on the front of the building. That door was never used until we added the front parking lot. We both chuckled at the logic.

We then built a beautiful sign in front with a flagpole and surrounding flower garden. The steeple was added after a 104-year-old lady died and donated the money. Part of her money was also used to bring in a professional landscaping company to put the finishing touches on the yard.

That was completed around my twentieth year as pastor, and that made us ready for major growth. The church was doing well, and growth was steady. The completed sanctuary sat around 275 people and we were averaging 200 people at our morning worship service. To grow any larger, we would have to go to two services on Sunday morning. We had arrived, but two services never happened.

The attendance topped out around 200. It then went down to 175, up to 185, down to 180, and up to 190. But we never went much beyond 200. Why? I loved to share God's Word. I loved seeing lives changed as people surrendered their lives to Jesus. I loved being used by God. But why didn't we become a large church? We were even willing to go to two services on a Sunday morning.

God had used me and directed me to help that church become a healthy church. I knew that, and I knew it was only through Him that we were spiritually, physically, and financially healthy. Plus, the congregation was made up of a special group of hardworking people.

That was about the time that leadership books and leadership seminars seemed to be everywhere. They seemed to support the theory that, by definition, church growth was dependent on leadership ability. I read a few books and realized their definition of a great leader was something I simply did not want to become.

I know I am oversimplifying their definition of a leader, but they seemed to define it to be someone with administrative qualities. An administrator was someone willing to take his or her hands directly off the people and then become a leader of secondary leaders who in turn touched people. The problem was, I did not want to lose contact with the people.

I learned this in a previous career as a salesman for adidas athletic shoes and apparel for the state of Michigan. I loved being a salesman and working directly with the store owners and purchasing agents.

In that position I was able to build strong relationships with them. I worked hard checking their inventory and then checking their backorders. I knew what their sales were for every model of shoe in stock. I even knew what sizes were selling best. It was my desire to make sure my product was making them money. I loved my job, and I loved helping stores make a healthy profit.

Because of that work ethic, my sales were strong—strong enough to gain recognition by the president of the company. He then asked me to become sales manager over a twenty-state area and forty sales representatives. That was a real honor, as it was a $100 million territory. I accepted.

It was a prestigious job. I flew to sporting goods shows all over the United States. Every week I flew to at least two different locations, sometimes even taking the corporate plane. I also flew to Germany for business meetings with the home office.

The experience was wonderful, but by the end of the first year I realized I hated the work. I was doing administrative work, making reports, and sending reports to the sales staff. I was only touching base with the sales staff and no longer with the store owners I had grown to care about. I was no longer able to directly help the stores become more prosperous, which brought me the greater joy.

Administration took me away from the work I enjoyed the most. I wanted to be on the ground level of sales, working with the people I loved, not working with people who would then work with the people I loved. God had gifted me at the entry level of sales, not the training level where I would train salesmen. After one more year as sales manager, I resigned and went back on the road.

Now let's go back to ministry. To become a greater church leader, I had to build a staff of secondary leaders and then spend time training and leading them. That would force me to spend less time visiting and encouraging the people I loved. I really enjoyed entry-level pastoring because God had gifted me in that level of ministry.

Late in my ministry I read a wonderful book titled *Living Your Strengths*. The book defined thirty-four areas of strength every person could potentially have. Then, after taking an online test, it defined the top five strengths God had given each person individually. I took the test and discovered the top five strengths God had given me. Administration was not one of them. The author then went on to suggest that we should develop our five strengths and become more efficient in each one of them. They were the five strengths that come easy to us because we are gifted in them. He also suggested we not try to develop an area that was not in our top five because that would take a lot of extra time and energy and give us weak and unsatisfactory results.

His theory was to understand and acknowledge our weaknesses and to bring someone alongside us to fill that role in our church. What a feeling of freedom that gave me. According to the leadership books on the market, I had to train myself to become an administrator because that was a skill I lacked. But according to the strengths book, I needed to develop the skills God gave me and then hire someone with administrative skills so our church could grow beyond two hundred.

I finally realized that four years before I retired, and for the last two years of my ministry I hired Craig, who was gifted in administrative skills. He did a wonderful job in that area, which gave me the freedom to do what God had gifted me to do. Unfortunately, it takes five years to see the results of a major change in a church, and I retired two years after the change. I never saw the results.

So why didn't God bring all that wisdom to me ten or fifteen years into my ministry instead of waiting twenty-six years? I could have been famous and possibly even had a TV ministry. The answer lies in the fact that God knew I was a pastor. One of my strongest skills was in pastoring, and that skill is defined as caring for people. It means being involved in the lives of people and caring about who they are and what they do.

I loved being a salesman and caring for the health of the stores and store owners that I called on. I loved being a pastor and entering into the lives of people in the congregation. I enjoyed church potlucks and the social aspect of sitting around a table and sharing in the lives of the people at that table. I enjoyed greeting people before and after church and hearing what was going on in their lives.

As the sales manager of a large corporation, I was not able to help the stores and store owners directly. As the pastor of a large church, I would not be able to personally be part of the lives of the people as well.

God knows what is best for me. He created me and gave me the very best. He gave me what He knew would be most gratifying and fulfilling in my life. At the age of seventy-three, I can look back over my life and see why I was never given the opportunity to be the pastor of a large church. I would have been miserable, even though I would have enjoyed the prestige of the position for a while.

I am now able to look back over my ministry and see God's hand in all of it. He started me out in the church I could enjoy the most. He gave me people who needed encouraging, some who needed to have a relationship with Jesus, and some who needed to be forgiven of their sins. He gave me a congregation that needed to be loved and needed a family outside of their biological family. God gave me the very best. He gave me a congregation whose needs fit my strengths. God is so good.

As another example, my daughter was tested and interviewed for a very high-paying job in the medical field. She got a rejection letter and felt awful. But after prayer and a time to consider the reasons, she realized the job would have put her in a small lab with no windows while she loves the outdoors. She would have also been processing test results for doctors and nurses. The problem is, she comes alive when she is around people, as she has a wonderful personality. That position did not fit her gifts and she would have been miserable. God wanted the very best for my daughter, and that new position was not on His radar screen for her.

Are we able to trust God and in what He gives us?

STUDY QUESTIONS:

1. Think about something you wanted to accomplish that never came about. Maybe it was something that made you feel disappointed with yourself.
2. Take time and think about some reasons why God may have kept you from doing that.

Chapter 12

God's Sense of Humor

Sometimes I visualize God looking down on us from heaven and just rolling with laughter. This may come when He sees us finally experiencing His love or joy for the first time. Love and joy have been available to us all along, and have even been in plain sight, but at the same time remain hidden from most of the world. Other times, He may roll with laughter when we have those *aha* moments, when we see Him working in our lives, doing what seems to be impossible things. This next story is one of those moments. I think He still chuckles when He thinks about it.

My son, Brad, was ready to purchase his first car. He had his eyes on a twenty-year-old Volkswagen bus that hadn't been driven or even moved in five years. Some friends of ours owned it, and I think Brad bought it for fifty dollars. It was a mess. It started right up, but the brakes were frozen, and we couldn't move it. On top of that, only first and second gears would engage. It's hard to back up a bus if only two forward gears work.

We finally broke it loose and pushed it backward so I could drive it home . . . very slowly. Did I mention that it also leaked a lot of oil? Home I went at twenty miles per hour, spewing oil all over the road and praying that the local police were having coffee and donuts so they wouldn't condemn the bus and declare it unsuitable to drive on any road.

I got it home, and the first order of business was to pull the transmission out and try to get all five gears working. In order to do that, we had to jack the back of the bus way up in the air and pull the engine and transmission out together from under the bus. We accomplished that major chore with the help of a neighbor. I took the transmission to a reputable shop, and they put it through all five gears with no effort. The mechanic said the transmission was in perfect running order. Great! We had spent almost a week trying to fix something that was in perfect working order.

We then discovered that the rod that connected the gearshift lever in the front of the bus to the transmission in the rear was frozen in one position and would not roll from left to right to engage all the gears. We should have known that because the gearshift lever itself would not roll from left to right. And God started giggling.

Next, before we put the engine and transmission back together and back into the bus, we investigated the oil leak. We washed the engine down completely, moved the crankshaft over and over, and could not find the leak to save our lives. We spent another whole day trying to pinpoint that problem only to find that the rubber funnel we poured the oil through to get to the engine had a crack in it. It was twenty years old and had rotted. And God giggled a little louder.

Over the next year, Brad got the bus on the road, and it ran quite well, even though it remained a very old vehicle. That summer he had secured a job at a Christian camp nine hours from our home in northern Wisconsin. He was determined to take the Volkswagen bus with him. Even though the bus was more than twenty-five years old and ran well, I would be hesitant to drive it much past the end of our driveway.

But what I thought really didn't count. He insisted on driving that old bus four hours up to the Mackinac Bridge, four hours west across the Upper Peninsula of Michigan, and then one hour into northern Wisconsin. Brad wanted to take his old bus on a nine-hour journey to camp, drive it around northern Wisconsin for the

God's Sense of Humor

summer, and then drive nine hours home in the fall. And he expected to do it without any mechanical trouble.

I argued with him for a couple days not to take it north. Brad, however, was determined to drive it to camp without my blessing. I warned him that if it broke down, he was not to call me. I was in the ministry, and it was a time in our life when we had no money left over after I paid the bills. I had no extra money to bail him out if he had any kind of mechanical failure.

Well, God was with Brad, and he easily made it to northern Wisconsin. But halfway through the summer, he decided it would be a good idea to overhaul the engine. He tore it apart and ordered the new parts he needed. I don't know how far away the new parts had to come, but in the end, that didn't matter. UPS went on strike. Old parts were lying all over the place and there was not a new part in sight. The engine could not be put back together.

Brad called me and asked if I could come get him and tow the bus home. He had to get home to attend college that fall. I was livid. Not only did I tell him not to take the bus up to camp and not to overhaul the engine five hundred miles from home, but I had also told him not to call me if he got in trouble. He called, and I told him to find his own way home. (As I write these words down, I really feel like an unfit father.)

When I hung up, my wife asked me what Brad wanted. She knew by the tone on my end of the conservation what he wanted, but I guess she wanted me to verbalize it. I did, and the conversation went something like this. "Now you listen to me. Your son needs your help and is asking for a favor. Get in your car and go get him—now!" I argued and argued with her, but all that came out of my mouth was, "Okay, dear." Just then I sensed that God smiled and said, "Good choice, Emerson."

I called different U-Haul dealers to rent a car hauler, and the only place I could find one was on the far western side of the Upper Peninsula of Michigan. I got in my car and set out to get my son and save my marriage.

By the time I left home, I only had seven hours to make an eight-hour journey to pick up the car hauler before the dealer closed for the weekend. I drove hard and furious. Once I crossed the Mackinac Bridge to get into the Upper Peninsula, I had no more freeways. I had to travel at an excessive rate of speed on a two-lane highway for the next four hours.

As I approached the U-Haul dealer I realized I was about forty-five minutes from the dealer with only fifteen minutes to make it before the dealer closed. It was impossible. I needed a miracle.

I began to pray and drive even faster, just hoping they would stay open an extra thirty minutes. If that didn't happen, I would have to spend two extra nights in a motel and wait until Monday morning to pick up the car hauler. I would have to find someone at the last minute to preach for me, which didn't sit well. I even talked to Brad a little, but of course he didn't hear me because he wasn't in the car. I knew I wasn't going to make it. It was up to God to perform one of His miracles. And then a miracle happened.

As I drove down that two-lane road faster than I should, I glanced off to my left and just happened to see a small roadside sign that read, "You are now entering Central Standard Time Zone." I couldn't believe it. When I passed that road sign, I gained an extra hour and I could easily get to the U-Haul dealer on time.

CENTRAL STANDARD TIME ZONE SIGN

"How long has that sign been there, God?

I looked up to heaven, smiled, and said, "God, did You just put that sign there, or has it been there for a while?" I could almost hear Him just rolling with laughter. That sign was put there more than a hundred years ago, but I think He just wanted to see me struggle for a few hours and then call out to Him in a panic. I'm sure He laughed and laughed at my discovery.

Maybe He was even disciplining me for the terrible way I treated my son that morning. Whatever it was, I'm sure He was enjoying my tense moments because He knew He could place that sign wherever He wanted it and whenever He wanted to. John 16:24 really fits this scenario well. It says:

> "Until now you have not asked for anything in My name. Ask and you will receive and your joy will be complete."

I asked, God answered with a chuckle, and my joy was great. Brad and I had a wonderful trip home. We enjoyed the beauty of God's creation and more than nine hours of meaningful conversation. I don't think I brought up anything negative the whole way home. I guess I was afraid that my wife might find out and discipline me again. I love it when God Laughs, even when it is at my expense.

STUDY QUESTIONS:

1. Consider a situation in your life that may have given God a good laugh.
2. Why do you consider it important to serve a God with a sense of humor?

Chapter 13

Remember

As I bring this book to its conclusion, the word "remember" is possibly the best word to summarize the message. It is a word that encourages us to look back in order to go forward, to remember the many times God intervened in our lives to give us faith that He will continue to intervene. We are to look back at the times God touched our lives and blessed us. Then we can look forward with confidence that the God we served back then is the exact same God we are serving right now and will serve in the future. When we *remember* how He touched our lives in the past, we can to be assured He will continue guiding us in the future. Then we can walk with greater faith and peace.

Moses used the word *remember* numerous times as he addressed the Israelites just before they entered the Promised Land. The nations they were told to conquer were stronger than they were. They had tall walls, that seemed impenetrable, protecting them. The nations were battle-ready, and that scared the Israelites. Some nations were even giants, descendants of the Anakites, and they heard that no one could stand up against the Anakites. Yet, in spite of their fear, they had witnessed the mighty hand of God numerous times as they traveled through the desert.

So, Moses began by reminding them of the powerful hand of the God they had served in the desert. God encouraged the Egyptians to let them go by performing ten powerful, miraculous acts. He provided food called manna in the hot and dry desert. He provided water for three million people in an arid and dry land. He provided clouds during the day to keep the hot sun from burning them and fire by night so they could find their way.

Their clothes didn't wear out for forty years, and their feet never swelled as they walked many miles. God parted the Red Sea and allowed them to escape from their enemy and then closed the sea as a huge army entered it to attack them. For forty years the Israelites experienced miracle after miracle.

The Promised Land was about to offer them the "good life," and Moses addresses them to help them remember the Mighty God who traveled with them, protected them, and guided them every step of the way. That's when Moses went into the *remember* oratory. Deuteronomy

7:17–19 describes part of the speech Moses shares with the Israelites:

> "Perhaps you will think to yourselves, 'How can we ever conquer these nations that are so much more powerful than we are? But don't be afraid of them! Just *remember* what the Lord your God did to Pharaoh and to all the land of Egypt. *Remember* the great terrors the Lord your God sent against them. You saw it with your own eyes! And *remember* the miraculous signs and wonders, and the strong hand and powerful arm with which He brought you out of Egypt. The Lord your God will use this same power against all the people you fear.'" (NLT)

Moses told the Israelites that the God who delivered them and led them for forty years through the wilderness was the same God who would be with them as they enter the Promised Land. *Remember* what He did so you will be confident in what He is able to do no matter what you face.

That is the essence of this whole book. As we look back over fifty, sixty, and even seventy years of our lives on this earth, we see the mighty hand of God protecting us, helping us through trial after trial, and teaching us through disciplinary actions what He can do.

Now, that God is the same God yesterday, today, and tomorrow. *Remember* that. Our trials and difficulties may change, but God will not change. If we can see His hand in our lives back then, we can expect He will deliver us no matter what we face. He may work miracles and deliver us in that manner, or He may allow us to go through a trial to experience His deliverance. He may also allow us to go through a trial just to learn a new life lesson or to experience His loving discipline.

Whatever the case, God has not changed. We may cry out in a moment of concern like King David did many times and say, "God, where are You?" But God will always be with us and help us to experience some form of victory. *Remember* what He did and then go forward with great faith, confidence, and enthusiasm. You can trust that God!

REMEMBER
REMEMBER
REMEMBER

And may the God of your past be the God of your future.

About the Author

Calvin L. Emerson is a retired minister. After receiving an engineering degree from Michigan State University, he designed and built custom vacation homes in northern Michigan. Later he became a salesman for adidas and then became sales manager for the same company. As a third career, he went into the ministry and remained at one church for twenty-eight years. He is spending his retirement years writing and speaking at camps and churches.

Author Calvin Emerson

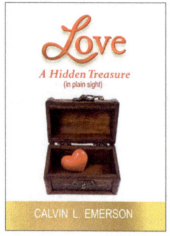
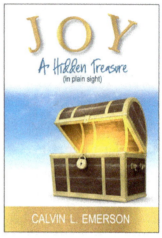
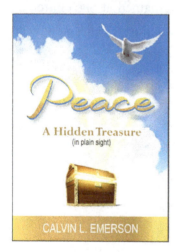
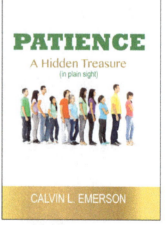

Other books the author has written

CPSIA information can be obtained
at www.ICGtesting.com
Printed in the USA
FFHW010747200819